Happy 70th Birthday!

Daddy,

Though you are a little bit older than the Thunderbird, your "class" far outshines these cars.

How we praise the Lord for each year of life you've been granted. We look forward to many more "29th" birthdays for you.

You're a wonderful daddy and the one and only, world's BEST Deedaddy!

Much love,
Donna, "J", JIM, Daniel

THE FORD
THUNDERBIRD

THE FORD
THUNDERBIRD

ROY BACON

GRAMERCY BOOKS
NEW YORK

This 2000 edition is published by Gramercy Books™,
an imprint of Random House Value Publishing, Inc.,
280 Park Avenue, New York, NY 10017,
by arrangement with PRC Publishing Ltd,
Kiln House, 210 New Kings Road, London, SW6 4NZ.

Gramercy Books™ and design are trademarks of
Random House Value Publishing, Inc.

Printed and bound in China

Random House
New York • Toronto • London • Sydney • Auckland
http://www.randomhouse.com/

A catalogue record for this book is available from the Library of Congress.

ISBN 0-517-16173-7

8 7 6 5 4 3 2 1

ACKNOWLEDGMENTS

The publisher wishes to thank the following photographers and picture libraries
for supplying the photography for this book:

Images on the front cover (all) and pages 3, 5 (top), 6 (top), 14 (top), 38 (bottom), 42 (both), 43 (both), 44 (both),
51 (bottom), 52 (both), 53, 56 (top and details, bottom), 57, 58, 59 (top), 60-61, 62, 64-65, 66, 67 (bottom),
72-73, 74, 75, 76, 77 (both), 78-79, 80 (bottom), 81 (both), 82-83, 84 (both), 85 (top), 96 (top), 106 (top) and
114 (top) supplied by Garry Stuart;
Images on pages 2, 4 (details, bottom), 21, 29, 35 (top), 46-47, 48, 51 (top), 88, 114 (details, bottom) and
115 supplied by Nicky Wright/NATMUS Museum, Auburn IN, USA;
Images on pages 6 (details, bottom), 7, 9 (both), 10-11, 12, 13, 17 (top), 25 (both), 26 (top), 31 (bottom), 34 (both),
50 (both), 54 (bottom), 55 (bottom), 63, 68 (top), 69, 85 (bottom), 88 (bottom), 94-95, 110, 116, 117, 118,
119 (both) and 128 (both) supplied by Tony Beadle Collection;
Images on pages 8, 14 (details, bottom), 15, 16, 17 (bottom), 20, 22-23, 27, 32-33, 36-37, 38 (top), 39 (both),
55 (top and middle), 59 (bottom), 66 (top), 86-87, 88 (top), 91 (top), 92 (both), 93 (all), 96 (details, bottom),
96-97 (main), 100-101, 103, 104-105 and 120-121 supplied by The National Motor Museum, Beaulieu;
Images on pages 18-19, 24, 26 (bottom), 28, 30, 31 (top), 35 (bottom), 40-41, 45 (both), 49 (both), 54 (top),
68 (bottom), 70, 71, 80 (top), 90 (both), 91 (bottom), 106 (details, bottom), 106-107 (main) and 111
supplied by LAT Photographic;
Images on pages 122, 123, 124, 125, 126 and 127 supplied by Ian Kerr;
Image on the back cover supplied by © AFP/CORBIS.

Contents

NEW NAME, NEW TYPE, NEW CLASSIC
— 1954   6

EARLY THUNDERBIRDS AND SQUAREBIRDS
— 1955 TO 1960   14

SIXTIES, SQUARES, ADDED DOORS
— 1961 TO 1969   56

PEOPLE, SIZE UP, SIZE DOWN
— 1970 TO 1979   96

SMALL AND AERO — 1980 TO 1988   106

FINAL DECADE, END, RESTART
— 1989 TO 2000   114

New Name, New Type, New Classic — 1954

The Thunderbird is an icon of the American auto industry. While it has changed form, style, and even purpose down the years, it has always kept its special nature and market niche.

At the start the T'Bird, as it soon became known, was a two-door, two-seat, sporting model, small by American standards, and built as a convertible with an optional hardtop that bolted into place. More of a roadster than an out-and-out sports car, it had styling links to main line Ford cars of its year. It was practical in use, well built, with a decent performance allied to a touch of luxury. It brought together some of the sports features common to European open cars with the general ease of operation that the American public had come to expect from a manufacturer they related to, trusted, and knew well.

The T'Bird evolved into different forms down the years but always remained special: a Ford and an American classic. Along with the style went the ongoing technical advances that kept the model at the forefront of the market.

The Thunderbird name came from the native American legends of the Arizona and New Mexico regions where it was believed that the bird ruled the skies to help mankind, and it was worshiped as a god. Winds, thunder, and the desert rain were created by the great wings, invisible to mortal man, and the improved climate that resulted brought prosperity to the tribes.

Right: Front corner of the new car as seen in 1954 when it still wore a chrome trim, borrowed from the Fairlane model, over the headlight.

Above: From the start — 1955 was the first production year — the Thunderbird looked right in its classic open two-seater form.

Above right: The Thunderbird was first seen at the Detroit Auto Show early in 1954 and went into the Ford line in the fall that year. Interest and demand were high from the start.

Bottom right: For many years the Thunderbird only fitted a V-8 engine. For 1955 this was of 292 cu. in. offering 193 or 198 bhp. (brake horsepower) when driving manual or automatic transmissions respectively. The chrome-plated air cleaner lid and cast-aluminum valve covers were part of an engine dress kit.

Ford was not alone in its use of the name. From late in 1949 the Triumph Engineering Company of Meriden in England had named its largest capacity motorcycle Thunderbird — it was a machine produced to meet the needs and demands of the American market, so the name was well established in the U.S. In requesting permission from Triumph to use the name on the new car, Ford stressed that the quality of the intended product would not impair the reputation and goodwill built up by the English company, and the use was agreed to.

The Thunderbird was born to meet the need that arose a few years after the end of World War II. In the early postwar days, car makers had to cope with the problems of both availability of manufacturing materials and the insatiable demands of a transport-hungry public. At first designs remained much as prewar — the demand was simply an unsophisticated desire for anything on four wheels — but once the immediate needs had been met, public perception of styles and marques moved on. The marketplace changed completely: marketing dominated what was chosen in the sales room. Style became the dominant factor, and in the early 1950s that meant streamlining and chrome-plating.

The mainstream cars of the early 1950s provided reliable transport all the year round, but were hardly exciting.

Right: This early publicity shot —
taken in 1954 — sums up well the
market sector chosen to promote
the new smaller and sporting car.

Above: Interior of the early Thunderbird: a bench seat for the two occupants, floor shift for the transmission, and an adjustable steering column.

Underneath the style, their brakes, handling, and road holding lagged behind that offered by European cars, built to run on very different roads to the long, straight highways of the U.S. A good number of Americans had sampled this alternative while serving abroad during the war and began to demand these features, combined with a more sporting package.

The result was a real increase in the size of the sports and roadster car markets to the point where sales figures rose to become significant to the major auto manufacturers. British firms such as Jaguar and MG were quick to oblige, but most of the imports to the U.S. were built in the pure sports car mode, and the U.S. market found them to be rather rough around the edges, lacking in the fixtures and fittings expected by many owners. This was fine for the enthusiast, but there was a much larger potential market for a roadster that offered both improved behavior and performance out on the road, while keeping the comforts most buyers were accustomed to.

Shows in Europe gave an indication of trends, and in the early-1950s senior Ford executives started to consider entering the market with a small sports car. Back in Detroit some staff were already putting ideas on paper, although without official sanction. The trigger came soon after, when Ford learned that arch rival

Chevrolet was planning to produce a two-seater sports car. It did so in 1953, when the Corvette made its debut and galvanized Ford into action — so much so that the Thunderbird was first shown at the Detroit Auto Show in February 1954. It was not until late that year that the T'Bird was first listed in the Ford line-up as a 1955 model, so the Corvette reached the market first. This was in part due to a simpler specification, and while both became cult cars with strong followings, they followed different paths from the start.

Ford, like Chevrolet, chose to make its first model a two-seater sports car but that was about the only similarity. The Thunderbird was designed to look like a Ford, used many stock Ford items out of the parts bins, and came with a steel body in a choice of colors, with a V-8 engine and manual or automatic transmission. The Corvette had its own style that did not relate to any other Chevrolet — a six-cylinder engine, automatic transmission without a manual option, and a fiberglass body that only came in white.

Above: Trunk space was limited for the first Thunderbird and much of it was taken up by the spare wheel. The trunk lid concealed the filler (gas) cap. When the trunk was shut a small hinged lid provided access.

Early Thunderbirds and Squarebirds — 1955 to 1960

In a sense the first Thunderbirds were conventional cars, even if a new departure for the firm founded by Henry Ford. They were conventional in that the body was built up from steel pressings welded into a structure and then assembled on the regular line along with the rest of the range. For sure they only had two doors, but so did other Ford models, including a convertible, while all manner of details were shared across the line.

The bodies actually came in the white, ready for paint and trim, from Budd Automotive, a long-established firm with an unrivaled reputation for the quality of its work. Into the body went a 292 cu. in., short-stroke, V-8 engine that would not reach the level of the rest of the range for a year. The quoted power output was 193 bhp. when coupled to a three-speed manual gearbox with floor shift and 198 bhp. for the Ford-O-Matic automatic transmission model.

Styling was American: simple and clean with an air scoop (an air intake that projects into the airflow to "scoop" a steady flow of air into the motor) on the hood, side vents ahead of the doors, limited chrome-plating, and covers to partly conceal the rear wheels. There were discreet rear fins to flank the trunk lid and a distinct Ford line which briefly included the side trim from the Fairlane model. Out of place on the T'Bird, it was not used in production although shown in early advertisements and installed on a few cars.

The base price was an excellent $2,944 which included some good features and included the fiberglass hardtop for the owner to bolt on as required. To this could be added power brakes and steering, the convertible top and extra trim while a choice of five external colors was offered.

"Thunderbirds are go," as the TV program would say, and so it was from the first public sighting of the car. Demand started

Right: The 1955 Thunderbird was of conventional construction, had a simple and clean line, and retained the good detail fitments expected by the U.S. market.

high and stayed there, so that over 16,000 were sold in the first year — in sharp contrast to the Corvette. Buyers preferred the larger engine, greater color choice, and steel body at a time when fiberglass was a new material and sometimes caused problems. They enjoyed the wind-up windows and the good fit of the top, keeping the American comforts they were used to while enjoying something different. It may not have been quite in the European image, but it was close enough, and came without leaks, rust, and doubtful electrics — the usual problems of so many imports, especially the sporting ones.

Ford left its successful sporting carriage well alone for 1956, dealing with the items that had brought customer complaints but also introducing a 312 cu. in. engine as an option. This gave 215 bhp. when used with the manual plus overdrive transmission and 225 bhp. with the automatic model. The 292 cu. in. engine ran on uprated to 202 bhp. with the three-speed gearbox. Later in the year, the 312 cu. in. motor was offered with a dual-quad carburetor that pushed the power up to 260 bhp.

There had been heat problems in 1955, particularly in the body cockpit floor area. To deal with this air vents were added just ahead of the doors. The modification improved the air flow through the passenger compartment, although it did not solve

Left: Fine shot of a 1955 convertible with the hood down. The Schlitz beer sticker on the trunk lid also appears in larger form on the left door and, presumably, the right one as well.

Above: Side view of the 1955 Thunderbird with the optional hardtop bolted in place, its finish matching that of the car. Raven Black, Thunderbird Blue, Snowshoe White, and Goldenrod Yellow were available, as well as this Torch Red.

the basic problem. The heat problem also affected the automatic transmission oil; to overcome this a pair of pipe lines was added to run the oil up to the radiator area where it had a chance to cool off.

Owners had found that the small trunk was inconveniently filled by the spare wheel, so this was moved into a continental carrier fixed to the rear bumper, a feature that had first appeared in 1955 as an after-market kit. The change did give much more room for luggage, but added inches to the car length and also affected handling, because the added weight was so far to the rear. Another complaint had been of wind buffeting for both driver and passenger; this was remedied by adding small deflectors to the screen pillars.

A noticeable change was the addition of a porthole to each side of the hardtop to remove a blind spot, improve visibility, and get more light into the car. The portholes also added to the style of the car and helped it to stand out from the crowd, but the original hardtop without portholes remained available to those who preferred them. A less obvious change, which affected the whole Ford range that year, was from 6-volt to 12-volt electrics, meaning new components in nearly all areas. For the interior, the steering wheel, dashboard, and some trim were altered to

improve safety and reduce personal injuries in the event of an accident.

There was a restyle and more engine options for 1957, when the spare wheel went back into a trunk that was had been extended and widened to take it. This removed the need for the external carrier, which allowed the rear fins to be sharpened in the manner of the time, while a new bumper and grille went at the front. The doors changed but the hood air scoop and body side vents remained, while the whole car sat lower to the ground thanks to a reduction in wheel size from 15-inch to 14-inch. This also aided the installation of the spare wheel in the trunk. The three tops continued as the hardtop with or without portholes, and the convertible which was available in rayon with a color choice or in white vinyl.

Under the hood the base specification continued with the 292 cu. in. engine uprated to 212 bhp. and a three-speed manual transmission. Overdrive and automatic transmission continued as part of the ever-longer option list and the 312 cu. in. engine was listed in several forms, starting with 245 bhp. using a four-barrel carburetor. Next was this engine with twin four-barrels and 270 bhp., these having an "E" in their code so the cars they went in became "E Birds." A 285 bhp. racing version was also

Above: For a contrast this 1955 car had the Snowshoe White finish for the hardtop and Torch Red for the body, a nice match that would stand out well anywhere.

Overleaf: The 1955 model had a floor-mounted lever to control the automatic transmission, and separate binnacles for the clock and rev-counter on either side of the speedometer, in this case reading to 240 and thus in kilometers.

available and finally there came a supercharged engine that powered "F Bird" cars with 300 bhp. on the street and more to come by tuning. These last were rare — barely 200 were built.

Late in 1957 the early form of the Thunderbird came to an end. It was time to move on from the two-seater sporting model to a larger form and market. In fact, Ford could sell all it could build but knew that the potential was limited. In three years the company had built over 53,000 T'Birds, far more than the Corvette had managed in five years although it was beginning to make up ground.

The Thunderbird was a success but a real increase in sales demanded that a rear seat be added so that owners could take out more friends. The result was a very different car whose style caused it to be known as the "Squarebird." It was altogether bigger and heavier with the wheelbase stretched from the original 102 inches to a useful, still compact, 113 inches. Onto this went a unitized body that was stronger than the older type, built up on a frame, and less likely to rattle and flex so the doors, hood and trunk lid would all have a better fit.

Hardtop and, from June 1958, convertible bodies were produced, still with just two doors. At the front went quad headlights under eyebrow lines that ran back along the sides, curved down

on the doors to spear forms, and then ran along them on to the rear bumpers. These spears were accentuated by hash marks applied on the rear of the door section.

The front bumper was massive, with small over-riders and a fine-mesh grille inset. The air scoop remained on the hood but was wider and shallower. For the rear there were quad taillights, each pair in its own housing, the license plate between them, and the trunk lid shaped down in the center to match. Tail fins remained and the square styling continued into the hardtop which no longer featured its portholes.

On the inside the bench seat of the first models gave way to twin bucket seats with a center console between them, a feature that would remain on the Thunderbird in some form or other from then on. This console kept the high drive-shaft tunnel out of sight so the new car could keep the low-slung line of the old, while the rear bench seat was styled to match the front pair.

For power there was just one engine, a larger 352 cu. in. V-8 pushing out 300 bhp. and driving the three-speed manual transmission, now with column shift, with overdrive and automatic options. A 430 cu. in., 350 bhp. engine was supposed to be listed but failed to be available.

Above left: The most obvious change for the 1956 Thunderbird was the relocation of the spare wheel into the continental carrier hung on the rear bumper, this an option kit for the first year.

Left: Showtime years later for a highly shined 1956 car, complete with its spare wheel carrier and still with the front bumper form copying the 1955 rear.

Above: The external spare wheel and carrier introduced for 1956 required a revised rear bumper which brought handling problems due too much extra weight too far back. It also made the car much longer.

Above: Small, adjustable air vents were added just ahead of each door for 1956 to provide some cooling for the passenger compartment lower area. There was a new front badge that year.

Right: Fine photo of a 1956 convertible. The driver side has a small wind deflector added to prevent buffeting and there should be one for the passenger.

Despite a general downturn in business in 1958, the new Thunderbird was an immediate success, with well over 35,000 hardtops plus over 2,000 convertibles being produced, well up on earlier years. This improved further in 1959 when some 67,000 were built in all, with around 10,000 as convertibles.

Changes for 1959 were mainly external, with a new grille of horizontal bars in place of the mesh and a revised bumper form. Arrowheads replaced the hash marks on the door spears with the "Thunderbird" script moved from its place just aft of the headlights to sit in the rear of the spear arrowhead. Underneath, the coil springs of the rear suspension changed to leaf springs, and the 430 cu. in., 350 bhp. engine became an option, but only with automatic transmission.

A variant built as a styling exercise had the top panel of the hardtop modified so that an area above each door hinged up as the door opened. This improved entry and exit, but at the cost of complication and a further series of joints to seal from the weather; it was not taken any further.

Yet another change to the grille came for 1960 with the bumper opening shallower and surrounding the mesh that carried a single horizontal bar across the middle and three vertical bars spaced across. Most of the other alterations were minor

Above: Rear aspect of a pair of 1956 T'Birds at a British show held in fine weather. The convertible has the correct wind deflectors and other features of the year.

Above right: Front aspect of the two 1956 cars showing the results that are possible given time, money, patience, and equipment. The hardtop has the porthole in the side which was added to remove the blind spot hazard.

Right: This could be the start of something long and costly. However, it is more complete than some, so a ground-up restoration could result in an award-winning car.

Overleaf: This 1956 car was modified by Pininfarina of Turin, Italy. It kept the side air vent and front bumper but not the spare wheel carrier or the side trim above the vents.

ones to the various pieces of body trim, so the spear arrowheads went and three hash marks appeared well back on the body sides. At the rear the twin taillights were replaced by triple light clusters, while the sighting details that had appeared on top of the front wings in 1959 changed form.

A welcome addition to the option list was a sunroof panel in the hardtop body. This was manually operated and gave the effect of an open car without the need to lower and stow the convertible top. From a total of 79,000 hardtops built that year around 2,500 had the sunroof option, while the convertible build was close to 12,000. The numbers showed that the T'Bird continued a popular buy, but also that customers for it appreciated its nature while retaining the comforts of the closed car, not the sporting image of the open one.

The last 1960 Thunderbird to come off the assembly line was very special for it had a stainless steel body. Still built by Budd, it was produced for Allegheny-Ludlum Steel Company as a promotional exercise and was seen by thousands at shows all over the USA. The buffed patina never changed and its schedule was a second tour in the year 2000 so thousands more could see that 40 years had no effect on stainless. Of course, it was expensive.

Above: The green body and white hardtop work well together for this 1956 car. That year brought 12-volt electrics and a number of safety improvements made in the passenger compartment.

Above right: For 1957 the body was restyled, although it remained a two-door, two-seater. It sat lower on 14-inch wheels, and most cars sold with the hardtop had the porthole version.

Far right: The frontal aspect of the T'Bird was revised for 1957, with a new bumper having the side lights built into it, while the grille became more noticeable.

Right: Interesting Thunderbird V-8 badge but not one to be found on the cars. It did appear on the Ford Fairlane models where the T'Bird engine option was fitted.

It was also the end of the line for Budd, as Ford itself began to produce the bodies in 1961. However, the link remained and in 1962 Budd was asked to produce a prototype of a two-seater T'Bird to take a version of the model back to its 1955 roots. Known as the XT-Bird, it was liked but not taken further, possibly because the Ford Mustang was not far from making its debut and going into much higher volume production.

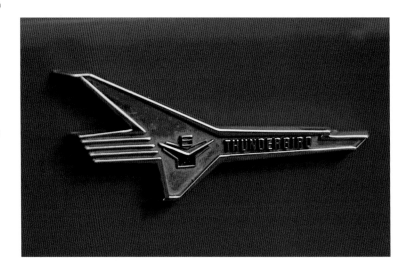

Right: A 1957 convertible with the top in place. The line was similar to the hardtop, but without the deep side panel that reduced visibility.

Above: Porthole hardtop model of 1957 with the new front end and sharper rear line. Red with white blends well with the whitewall tires and thin red wheel trim line.

Right: The Thunderbird script sat on the side of the tail fin for the first two years, but in 1957 moved to forward of the side vent trim, a radio aerial just above it.

Above: One minor change for 1957
was to the fuel filler cap that moved
to the right side of the body rear
where it lived under a hinged
cover lid.

Left: Front end for 1957 remained
staid by some U.S. standards with
limited use of trim or chrome
plating. The air scoop remained on
the hood and there were more
options to go under it.

Overleaf: An interesting hybrid, this
vehicle has a 1957 model front end
but carries its spare wheel on an
earlier, external mounting. Other
features, however, confirm the 1957
origins. (See also pages 42–44.)

More views of this interesting 1957
hybrid.

Above: The rear end reveals how
the tail was modified to mount the
rear bumper further back to
accommodate the spare wheel.

Right: This front detail shows the
hood over the headlights as usual,
but with a chrome-plated bezel in
place of the usual body color; also
the side light detail.

Above: The engine bay shows a 292 cu. in. V-8, which was fitted as standard; a 312 cu. in. unit was available in various forms. The chrome-plated air cleaner lid and finned valve covers were part of the engine dress kit.

Left: The speedometer position was changed in 1957 to a position directly in front of the driver, flanked by the minor dials, while the automatic transmission lever remained on the floor.

Above: Close-up detail of the cast-aluminum valve cover, with cooling fins and manufacturer and model names. It and the plated items were part of the dress kit.

Right: Tail detail of the hybrid that kept the standard light and fin, only the external spare wheel not conforming.

Above: A 1957 hardtop model with porthole on show in the sunshine in later years. Such events enable owners and enthusiasts to exhibit their cars and the public to view and enjoy.

Left: For 1958 the first of the four-seat Thunderbirds was unveiled with a completely new style that was soon known as the Squarebird. Here, it goes on show.

Overleaf: The new T'Bird was much longer and heavier than the old, but retained the two-door layout for both the hardtop and this convertible version. The hash marks on the door spear were a recognition feature.

Far left: The front of the Squarebird was more aggressive than the earlier cars with a massive bumper that enclosed the grille. Above sat the quad headlights under eyebrows, more new features.

Above: Separate front seats with a center console plus a twin-pod dash were new for 1958. Air conditioning was standard, its controls on the console and outlet vents above the radio.

Left: On show in the Netherlands, the new car revolved to show off its lines in hardtop form. Just one engine was listed, a 352 cu. in. V-8.

Above: The lever for the automatic transmission moved to the steering column for the Squarebird to complement the new interior style and layout.

Right: Material from the 1959 brochure, the year when the door spear gained a plated arrowhead. The name script also moved to the door spear from the front fender.

Far right, Above: A 1959 convertible with the top in place. For that year the front grille was changed to horizontal bars and the hood scoop became a dummy.

Far right, Below: The sheer length of the Squarebird has been accentuated on this car by the addition of the spare wheel carrier. The trunk lid was power raised and lowered as was the top.

Above: The Squarebird sat on a 113-inch wheelbase, still quite acceptable, but the overall length went up by 24 inches even without the addition of the external spare wheel.

Right: Rear corner detail for 1959 when, as for 1958, twin taillights in a single assembly went on each side with the license plate between. For 1960 there would be three smaller lights on each side.

Far right: Front corner detail for 1959 showing the paired headlights under their eyebrow, the side light set in the bumper, revised grille and the fender top mark whose insert changed from black to clear for 1960.

Above: A 1959 convertible on show in Europe with the top down. The Edsel name was one that Ford would want to forget with just three unsuccessful production years.

Right: Part of the 1959 brochure showing the convertible with the top down to give a view of the general layout of the interior, both front and rear.

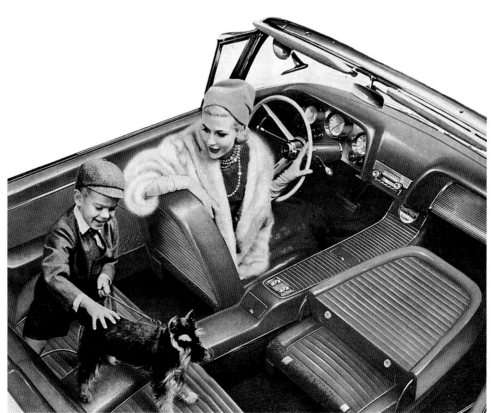

Above: A 1959 hardtop on show in Europe with either a salesman or a potential buyer weighing it up. Their thoughts would run along very different lines.

Left: The 1959 convertible was an impressive car from all angles and could be fitted out from the option list to make it individual to its owner.

Below left: For 1960 there was another change to the grille with one horizontal and three vertical bars, a new front badge, no arrow-heads and three hash marks on the rear sides.

Sixties, Squares, Added Doors — 1961 to 1969

It was all change for 1961 with the differences as drastic as when the Squarebird replaced the original two-seater. The space age of the Sputnik, rockets, and the race to the moon had dawned and was reflected in automotive styling. The Thunderbird had to be in the lead of this trend and the design went through several stages before being released.

Some of the restyle came from the X-100 project car that had been shown in 1955 with futuristic front and rear ends, along with the large hardtop side panels that were common to many T'Birds. At first the line for the Sixties was too advanced to be acceptable, with a bullet nose, jet engine outlet tail, and rocket fins. Viewed against the evolution of the Squarebird, it had moved too far from the staid to the comic book, but once revised it became fresh, new, and innovative. In the process the nose was amended several times, but in the end it remained pointed in side view and this style later appeared in Britain on the Ford Corsair.

The quad headlights stayed, but sat lower and were incorporated in the grille and bumper line from where the body sides ran back cleanly and without the sculpted forms of the past. A single line ran from the nose along the top edge to end in a modest fin at the rear. The scripted name went on the side of the nose, ahead of the front wheel, and the hash marks became horizontal lines that remained at the rear. The air scoop in the hood moved forward and adopted a vee form. At the rear there were just two large, circular taillights set at either end of the bumper to simulate jet engine or rocket motor outlets.

Hardtop, no longer with the sunroof option, and convertible models were offered, and the new styling gave both a clean line,

Right: Nose detail of the 1962 model.

Above: The 1961 Thunderbird was all new from end to end, clean from the front to the modest tail fins. Its style would run for three seasons; this is a 1962 model.

Above right: A Convertible Sports Roadster model was added for 1962. This had a detachable fiberglass tonneau cover over the rear seats to convert the car back to the earlier two-seat form: neat but costly.

Bottom right: Thunderbird development with the new 1961 hardtop at front, a 1957 convertible at center, and a 1960 Squarebird hardtop with sunroof at the back.

Overleaf: Little was altered at the front end for 1962 in view of the major changes of the previous year. The strong link across the front between the headlights was used on other Ford models.

free from the contrasting features of the past that sometimes opposed each other to detract from the overall effect. Among the many options was a movable steering wheel that could be swung away to increase clearance for entry and exit. Popular, it was standard for 1962.

Under the hood went the familiar V-8 engine, but enlarged to 390 cu. in. although the power stayed at 300 bhp. The larger engine options were dropped along with the manual transmission, for times were changing and automatics were becoming the norm. It would be two decades before the Thunderbird would again have a clutch and manual gearshift.

In all, the new style made its mark and a gold convertible was chosen as the pace car for the Indy 500 race that year, the 50th Anniversary for that event. However, production numbers were down, although 73,000 was far better than the early days when the Thunderbird only had two seats.

Little was altered to the style for 1962 although the trim lines on the rear quarter were changed to a trio of hash marks in line astern. An uprated version of the 390 cu. in. engine appeared as an option, with 340 bhp. on tap thanks to having three two-barrel Holley carburetors in place of the single four-barrel, a raised compression ratio, special air cleaner with less restriction on the

Above: The space under the hood was more congested by 1961 but the dresser kit, mainly plated items, continued to be listed while the 390 cu. in. engine was the standard fitment with an option available to offer extra power.

air flow, and some chrome-plated items to brighten up the under-hood scene. However, there were not many takers for the package.

More important was the introduction of two new versions of the Thunderbird to join the existing pair. The first was the Convertible Sports Roadster that was aimed to satisfy buyers who preferred a two-seat open car. This was achieved by fitting a fiberglass tonneau cover over the rear seats. It was styled to fit to the backs of the front seats in the manner of racing headrests. In addition, there were Kelsey-Hayes wire wheels, for which the rear wheel covers had to be removed to give clearance. A grab rail was provided for the passenger, and suitable special badges fitted to the body sides at the front. The added tonneau flowed nicely into the style to give the T'Bird a more sporting line. If four seats became essential, it could be removed, and even when in place the soft top could still be raised or lowered. It certainly had the style, but it was a good deal more expensive than the convertible so sales were slow in 1962 and much slower for the next and last year. After then the parts were offered as accessories but there were few takers, most buyers seeming to prefer to keep to the four seats and spend their money on items from the option list.

More successful was the Landau version of the hardtop. It had a vinyl-covered roof and a Landau bar on each side of the top to the rear of the door. The interior had an improved trim and, at only $77 more than the stock model, it sold better and better as the years went by.

The whole range ran on for 1963 with a minor change in the body style, thanks to a line that ran along the sides from the headlights to the door where it curved down. Just below it, on the door, three hash trims appeared, while those at the rear were replaced by the scripted name. Otherwise the line-up was as before, but with one special limited edition — the Monaco Landau, named after the town in which it was first shown to the public. Just 2,000 were built, each with a numbered plaque on the console panel, and they were finished in white with a non-standard color for the roof. The same colors were used for the seats and carpets, the landau side bars were special, and wheel covers that simulated knock-off hubs were fitted.

During 1963 two Thunderbird show cars were seen, the Constellation and the Italien. Both were in the fastback style with the roof line carried much further back before it ran down to the trunk at a shallower angle than usual. Cars such as these evoked interest at shows and won publicity for the firm so were by no

Above: A 1962 hardtop standing next to a Chrysler of the same period that featured slanted quad lights. The light body color was just one of a dozen or more listed by Ford.

Overleaf: The interior was revised for 1961 but continued with separate front seats and the center console carrying the air conditioning unit; the radio was now at the top

means uncommon. More plentiful, but not for the public eye, were the styling models built as exercises for evaluation but fated just to be stages in the process from paper ideas to production.

For 1964 the style went back to the more conservative Squarebird form, as the rocket version had seen sales fall off. The change brought the eyebrows back over the quad headlights, and sculpted body sides in a less aggressive form than before — discreet rather than flamboyant. The front bumper, grille, and hood were all new, as were the rear bumper and trunk lid, while the line of the windows was amended. At the rear the round taillights were replaced by rectangular ones to give a totally different line.

The 300 bhp., 390 cu. in. engine and automatic transmission ran on to propel the car, and there were no options. On the inside the story was different, for bucket seats took the place of the earlier, bulky items, and the rear seat back was altered to curve each end of the outer section in the style of a couch. This enabled a single passenger to gain extra leg room by sitting partly sideways which made it a neat point in the salesroom, although such a posture could lead to a painful back.

New that year for the hardtop was "Silent Flo" ventilation that relied on the external air flow over the body to encourage

the stale air to move out and fresh air in. The Convertible and Landau models continued, but the Sports Roadster was dropped. For those customers who still sought that type, there remained a fiberglass tonneau cover available as an option for either the dealer or customer to fit. Most who bought it also had the sporting Kelsey-Hayes wire wheels which were an option for all models.

An important, although out-of-sight change for 1965 was the adoption of front disc brakes, which gave the car much better and safer stopping power. Another safety item was to modify the turn signals at the rear so that each segment came on in turn, working from the inside bulb, until all were on, thus attracting the attention of following drivers more readily.

On the outside the front grille was amended and there were minor trim changes. The model name on the leading edge of the hood was replaced by a badge, as was that between the taillights, while new trims went on the body sides behind the front wheels and ahead of the doors to simulate air vents. The three models ran on as before but without the tonneau cover option and there was a limited edition Special Landau with its own finish while the engine and transmission were unchanged.

Above: British registration for this 1963 convertible with its top down. It shows the style line added that year to run straight back and then curl down behind the door hash marks.

Above left: The three hash marks advanced from the tail to the door for 1963, while the model name script moved from the nose to the tail. This hardtop had the external spare wheel.

Left: A Landau hardtop was introduced for 1962 with a vinyl-covered roof and styled bars on each side of the top. The interior trim was improved and its small extra cost resulted in good sales.

Sales had dropped in 1965 so there were moves to correct this for 1966. Output of the stock engine was raised to 315 bhp. and a larger 428 cu. in., 345 bhp. unit was added as an option. The hardtop and convertible continued to be listed but the Landau was replaced by the Town Landau that was joined by the Town Hardtop. These two Town models had the upper side panels of the body brought further forward to the rear edge of the door. This gave the models a more distinguished line and enhanced rear seat privacy, but did create a blind spot, much as with the first hardtop that had led to the porthole style of 1956.

For the rest, the 1966 cars had the front end cleaned up with hood, grille, bumper, and headlight surrounds all changed to create a more unified assembly with a touch of aggression. The simulated air vents came off the body sides to clean up that area and the taillight became one unit stretching right across the car within the rear bumper.

It was the last year of the convertible, for sales of that type were well down and had never matched those of the hardtop. In addition, there was new safety legislation in the government pipeline which would be hard for the convertible to conform with without major changes; additionally, the Thunderbird had moved on from its early, sporting image. It was now centered on

the market sector that desired the comforts offered by most cars, allied to a personal touch with a hint of luxury thrown in for good measure. It was a car that would stand out from the crowd just enough to make a statement about the owner.

Some of this had been seen in show models such as the Golden Palomino of 1964 and the Apollo of 1967, of which five were built at considerable expense. Features, often with revisions, from these hardtops found their way into production as part of a complete restyle for 1967, while the mechanics remained as they were.

The major change to the line for that year was the appearance of a four-door Landau alongside the two-door hardtop and Landau models. All had a longer wheelbase, up by 1.5 inches for two-doors and four inches for the four-door. Construction went back to the body-on-frame of the early cars and both inside and out had a new line.

At the front a wide mouth above the bumper enclosed a mesh grille that had vacuum-operated doors at each end to conceal the quad headlights until they were needed. A large model badge went in the center, while the bumper was formed to run across the car, under the grille, and then up at each side to match to the front of the body panels. The lower body edge was

Above: Non-standard minor changes for this 1963 British-registered hardtop were the name script on the hood and the small badge ahead of the front wheel that was only used by factory cars for 1962.

Overleaf: Squarebird styling returned for 1964 as the fashions swung again in response to public demand. However, the wheelbase and overall length stayed as they were.

Above: Rear view of the 1964 convertible that had a new line in rectangular lights set within the chrome-plated, one-piece housing with the model name in the center.

highlighted by trim pieces that ran along each side: first from the bumper to the front wheel, second between the wheels, and third from the rear wheel to the new rear bumper. This trim underlined the car and a formed body line above it that ran from the top edge of the front bumper to the rear one. At the wheel arches the line was taken up to follow the arch line before continuing along the body.

The wheels themselves had a new style of cover with a radial spoke design, while the rear wheels were no longer partly hidden by separate covers, these having begun to go in the previous year. While often popular with stylists, these detachable panels could be less so with dealers and owners, as the panels had a tendency to drop off along the road or refuse to come off when removal was needed to change a tire. In some cases they were prone to corrosion, so few tears were shed when they went.

On the inside there were many changes, affecting console, instruments, dashboard, and trim, and there were new seats with a bench at the front in place of the individual buckets. To improve safety in the cabin there was a new steering wheel center with impact-absorbing padding, and to help to avoid accidents there was a dual-circuit braking system. No longer would a simple failure leave the driver without brakes.

The new body styles had some unusual features, with the four doors of the longer Landau hinged at the front and rear respectively. Thus, they met in the center in a style that had gone out of fashion prewar when it was realized that the rear hinge was no asset if a door accidentally opened while the car was in motion. Small, European cars sometimes had this arrangement without the center pillar to aid access but this hardly applied to a car of U.S. proportions.

The four-door Landau had a rear bench seat of more usual form, although the type with curved ends continued on the two-door models. These had a further unusual feature in that their rear quarter lights moved to the back into the upper side panels rather than down behind the door when they were opened.

In all, Ford had reason to be pleased with its revised model line: the new four-door sold well and the sales total was up from the previous year. The three models continued on for 1968 with minor changes, although the bucket front seats did return as an option. At the front a coarser mesh grille took over, minus the center badge but plus a smaller one on each headlight door.

Reflectors appeared on the body sides at front and rear just below the formed body line, with turn signals just ahead of them at the front. The three-part trim that underlined the body was

Above: The body lines ran directly from front to rear for the 1964 cars, one along the upper edges and the other just above wheel-center height.

Above: Detail of the front corner with its paired headlights and their eyebrow that ran back into the upper body style line. Beneath is part of the new front bumper.

made much thinner and under the hood the 390 cu. in. engine made way for the 428 cu. in., with the new 429 cu. in. that produced 360 bhp. an option.

Further show cars were built after the Apollo — the Saturn and Saturn II were both modified hardtops and seen in 1968 and 1969. Both were sleeker than the stock models with more of a European fastback line. As usual, some of their features found their way onto later production cars.

For 1969 the front grille changed again to a die-cast part with the mesh highlighted by a heavier horizontal bar plus three vertical ones. The front badge went back into the grille center and an additional pressing was added beneath the bumper as a splash guard. Along the body sides the bottom trim gained a rib, while the rear side reflectors were much reduced in size. At the rear, twin taillights replaced the single unit with the reversing lights in a panel between them.

The two-door hardtop continued with its rear quarter light, but this went from the two-door Landau that had the upper side panels lengthened to suit. Both Landaus saw the return of the factory sunroof option, now electrically operated instead of manually as in the past. The list of options grew ever longer while many items that had once been options became standard

equipment as the specification became fuller and more luxurious. One that went was the 429 cu. in. engine, for that became the standard and only fitment, while among the standard details was an automatic parking brake release.

However, sales were down as the Thunderbird lost out to opposition from other makes, and even another Ford or two. Thunderbird sales were about to go through a lean time.

Above: The extensive mechanism that raised and lowered the hood caught midway with the trunk lid open to allow the hood passage. Clever design enabled it to work well and reliably.

Below left: The 390 cu. in. V-8 engine producing 300 bhp. powered the 1964 cars well enough, so there were no options in that area. It tucked in neatly along with its accessories.

Overleaf: This photograph emphasizes the length and rear overhang of the convertible. In this case, the vehicle is fitted with full wheel trims with simulated knock-off hubs, and so is minus the wheel covers to avoid masking the shine.

Above: A Landau hardtop from 1964
when a new ventilation system was
adopted that used the outside air
flow to move the internal by placing
extraction vents at low-pressure
points.

Right: The sheer size of the 1964
Thunderbird was more pronounced
when seen from above. Bucket seats
were new that year, as were the
curved corners of the rear seat.

Above: A ribbon speedometer was adopted for 1964 with four minor dials beneath it. The Swing-Away steering wheel was fitted to this car, a popular option that eased entry and exit.

Left: A further view of the 1964 seating where the rear seat curve allowed a single passenger to gain legroom by sitting part sideways. This was a useful point in the sales room but the result was hardly comfortable.

Overleaf: More general view of the 1964 interior showing the center console extended to the rear compartment, which hardly helped sideways sitting. Only automatic transmission was available.

Above: Detail of the 1964
speedometer reading up to
120 mph., and the four minor dials,
switches, levers, and radio in the
center.

Right: The small dials read from
the left: oil, fuel, temperature, and
generator charging. The usual
automatic transmission selections
were controlled by the lever on
the right.

Above: Rear view of the 1964 car with its rectangular lights and the model name above the license plate — a major restyle from the round lights of the past.

Left: Fine 1964 convertible in Britain where such cars are much appreciated by enthusiasts for the American way of motoring, even if they do not always fit the roads.

Overleaf: The front grille was revised to add vertical bars for 1965, as seen on this convertible with the top in place. The other models with this revision were the hardtop and the Landau.

Above: This photograph shows the 1965 convertible on page 86–87 with the top down and furled. An identification feature for 1965 was the simulated vents on the body sides between the front wheel and the door, only used for that one year.

Left: A new badge replaced the block letters of the model name on the hood for 1965 only, and a similar change was made to the area between the taillights.

Far left: Interior of the 1965 model that was little altered from the previous year when it was fully revised. It is neat and tidy and still has the center console.

Above: For 1966 the front end was cleaned up with changes to the hood, grille, bumper, and headlight surrounds, giving a more unified and aggressive line.

Above left: The major change for 1965 was to the chassis with the adoption of disc brakes for the front wheels, a welcome and useful improvement in that area.

Far left: A pair of 1965 Thunderbird convertibles with British plates. As for the previous year, there was only one engine listed and all models had the automatic transmission.

Left: Interior of the 1966 hardtop that retained the rear quarter windows not featured on the Town models. It kept the style first seen in 1964, well appointed and comfortable.

Top: The hood badge moved onto the new grille for 1966, when the hood became longer and its scoop flatter. The bumper was new and this is the Town Landau with the extended upper side panel.

Above: : Stock hardtop for 1966. The dummy side vents were no longer fitted and the taillights and bumper became one assembly across the rear of the car.

Above: A major restyle was carried out for 1967. The main news was the addition of a Landau with four doors, a first for the model line. It continued to feature the side bars and vinyl roof .

Left: Wheel covers were dropped for 1967, and the grille was changed to conceal the quad headlights under twin doors that revealed them when needed. This is a 1968 model.

Below left: Despite the safety interests that were becoming more prevalent, the four-door Landau had the rear doors hinged at the rear in the style of the 1930s and not a safety feature.

Right: The twin, small grille badges
indicate a 1968 two-door Landau,
the 1967 models having a single
large badge in the grille center. This
is an impressive car fitted with the
optional wheel trims.

People, Size Up, Size Down — 1970 to 1979

Right: Bold, aggressive, and forthright front end of the 1970 Thunderbird that was not to all tastes and had a mixed reception from Ford dealers and public alike. A 429 cu. in. V-8 engine went under the hood.

The 1970 Thunderbird had a new, thrusting style brought about by Semon Knudsen, who had moved over to Ford from General Motors. He arrived early in 1968, too late to alter the 1969 line, but with a clear year to stamp his personality onto the cars for the next decade.

The main change was to the front end of the existing line of hardtop and two- or four-door Landau models that retained the sunroof option. In place of the simple shape, with its grille and concealed headlights, came a pronounced and aggressive center section in the form of a forward pointing vee. The grille was shaped to suit this and flanked by separate frames

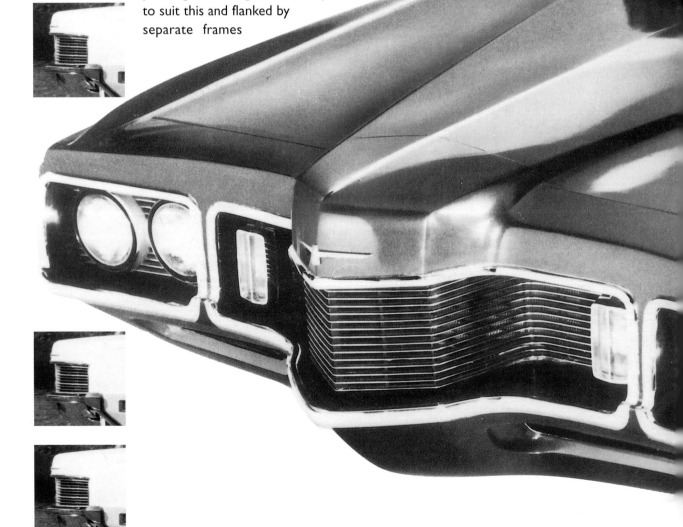

on each side for the twin headlights. The under panel became, in effect, the front bumper, and the rest of the body ahead of the doors was revised to suit the new form. At the rear the taillight was back to a new, full-width design, and the side reflectors, turn signals, and bottom side trim were all amended. The engine remained the 429 cu. in. unit without any options.

The new style had a mixed reception from Ford dealers and the sales volume was only a bare 1,000 above 1969. Knudsen was none too concerned, for he was busy altering other Ford models and the upshot was his removal from the firm late in 1969. His replacement was Lee Iacocca, who was equally forceful and had been angling for the position before, but at first his plans were curtailed by lack of funds as Knudsen had spent more than his allocation.

For 1971 Iacocca left well alone, so the line and its mechanics ran on with some horizontal strips added to the front grille, revised front bumper, new wheel covers, and some trim changes. Sales dropped further to around half the 1967 total to make it only too clear that the firm had taken a wrong turn.

The route that Iacocca chose to follow to remedy and correct this situation was that bigger was better. Now well away from the original Thunderbird sporting concept, the new car was planned to be the Ford flagship, loaded down with style, comfort, fixtures, luxury, and with a long option list so that no customer lacked for choice or would be afraid to look all in the eye once out on the road.

Behind this thinking there was also a need to update the Lincoln Continental, another Ford model that Iacocca carried responsibility for, and one that would take too much money to improve for a fast return. The answer was to share costs with the Thunderbird and use the same platform and body parts with them dressed up to suit their markets. It worked, too, so the 1972 Thunderbird was only offered in the two-door hardtop form but with a very long line of options and a wide range of colors. These included a Glamor Paint line that had a special brilliance and introduced some color-coded features as part of the option.

Under the body the car rode on new all-round coil-spring suspension with a four-bar-link location at the rear. The stock engine continued to be the 429 cu. in. unit with the power output set down to a real 212 bhp. measured using the required SAE (Society of Automotive Engineers) methods. These called for the readings to be taken from the engine as installed in the car and not, as had been Detroit practice, with most of the ancillaries removed and the settings adjusted to maximize the numbers. The horsepower race had seen the tests run with air cleaner, generator, cooling fan, water pump, and even the oil pump removed or run externally to the test. The ignition and carburetor settings would be adjusted to suit each engine speed but real life had finally caught up with all the firms. The engine option was a 460 cu. in., 224 bhp. unit that was a standard fitment when the air conditioning system was installed.

During 1972 Thunderbird production went past the one million mark and that one had a white vinyl top and general gold finish with special badges to commemorate the event. It was bought for a private collection and went to stand next to a 1955 car where it emphasized the 1,500 lb. weight gain and 40-inch length increase. The Thunderbird had grown into a big car with the wheelbase up to 120.4 inches and the weight to over 4,500 lb. The sporting feel was long gone.

However, despite the car's appetite for fuel, it sold well — close to 58,000 units, which was more than 20,000 above the 1971 figure. It did even better in 1973, when the total went over 87,000, although the changes were relatively minor. However, one that was mandatory was to meet legislation that required the car to withstand a 5 mph. front-end collision without damage to any safety-related parts. This was done by modifying the bumper and its mountings but added further to the weight.

As usual, the grille was altered and changed to an egg-crate form from the horizontal bars of the previous year, while each of the four headlights now had its own housing so they were no longer in pairs. Above the grille the model badge was replaced by the name itself in block letters, and the car continued to be well equipped inside and out as standard. The sides had the body line emphasized much more with the addition of further trim along its length to enhance it.

A useful feature added for 1973 was an opera window in each upper side panel to give the appearance of the Lincoln Continental and improve visibility, just as with the portholes in the past. From the middle of the year they became a standard fitting along with power windows, vinyl roof, and tinted glass, but this still left a long option list.

Little that was obvious appeared for 1974, when the rear bumpers fell under the mandatory collision requirement and the ever-increasing weight caused the firm to use the 460 cu. in. engine as the stock unit, rated at 220 bhp. Legislation brought in a seat belt interlock system that forced drivers to buckle up before the engine could be started, and proved a real nuisance in some circumstances. Owners bypassed the system and the general public complained bitterly of government intrusion, so the whole matter was soon dropped.

Above: Major style changes came
for 1970, mainly to the front end
although the line of the roof of the
two-door model was flattened out
and smoothed as well.

There was still only a single model, the two-door hardtop,
that continued to be offered with the sunroof option. A second
option substituted glass for the steel sunroof and was listed as
the moonroof, a neat touch. At the rear went revised taillights
with four sections to each side of the reversing light panel, and
the new and massive rear bumper beneath their housing.

Times were changing with the oil embargo late in 1973, and
the effects of this could be seen in a drop of 30,000 units in
Thunderbird sales. Emission laws also increased fuel consumption as well as lowering performance, so big was no longer beau-
tiful and some major changes were needed. However, it was
never easy to shed weight and size quickly, so the existing model
had to run on for two more years.

In 1975 the 460 cu. in. engine was further derated to a mere
194 bhp., while Ford pushed the luxury theme to move product
out of the showroom. The long list of standard fitments that
were extras on other cars was heavily promoted, as was the continuing lengthy option list available to further gild the lily.

It was the 20th Anniversary of the Thunderbird that year
which gave marketing a further handle to use, and on this was
hung two special packages, the Copper Luxury Group and the
Silver Luxury Group. For the first the car was finished in white

or Copper Starfire, with the copper color continued on for
other items. There were special opera windows and brighter
wheels, while on the inside the copper theme was continued into
the upholstery, carpets, and trims. The second package was much
the same with the car painted in Silver Starfire but with a choice
of silver or red for the interior.

Sales still continued to fall so even more luxury was piled on
for 1976. The result was a fine car that embodied everything that
the Thunderbird had come to mean in that period. No less than
three special luxury packages were on offer to personalize the
vehicle, these being the Creme and Gold, the Bordeaux, and the
Lipstick. Ostentation seldom came better, especially for the first
of these, specially tailored for extroverts. The engine power crept
up a little to 202 bhp. while some 850 lb. of weight was shed. Four-
wheel disc brakes became an option while the anti-lock brake system, first offered as a 1972 option, continued to be listed.

Sales did pick up for 1976 but this may have been because it
was clearly the last chance to buy that type of car. The times
demanded something smaller, lighter, and a good deal less thirsty,
but there were always those that craved a big, luxurious car.
Never mind the fuel bills and the headaches in heavy traffic, the
largest Thunderbird made a clear statement about its owner.

Of course it had to change. New legislation required reduction of harmful emissions and improved occupant protection. To pay for this by increased sales' volumes was impossible for such a massive luxury model without a price rise that would take the model out of its established class.

A very different Thunderbird appeared for 1977, much leaner and lighter with 10 inches shaved off the length, 6.4 inches from the wheelbase, and 700 to 800 lb. down on the weight. It was based on a mid-sized platform shared by a number of models in the Ford range with sufficient variations in the way the parts were combined to make the final results work.

This was especially so for the Thunderbird which kept to its two-door hardtop form as the base model, with a Town Landau that carried much, but not all, of the option list for the deluxe end of the market. The style was fresh, with a coupe top that was highlighted by a band that ran across the top and down each side to the waist line. This gave the car a Targa style, the name relating to one of the top European sports car races and a form found on several high-performance models from Germany and Italy.

The band was more than a decoration, for it added to the rigidity of the structure and sat well between the door windows and new rear quarter windows that greatly enhanced visibility. The opera windows continued as a feature, but were turned so their length was in the vertical plane which allowed them to fit within the side band.

To power the new, lighter Thunderbird there was a choice of three engines, all still of the V-8 form so common in America. The base version was of 302 cu. in. developing 130 bhp. through a two-barrel carburetor — except for California where a 351 cu. in. offering 135 bhp. was stock and an option elsewhere. Top of the engine line was a 400 cu. in. option generating 173 bhp. and fitted as standard to the Town Landau which weighed 200 lb. more than the hardtop before the customer began to consult the option list.

The models were as well equipped as Thunderbird owners had come to expect, at a very reasonable base price of $5,063. Of course, this was without options, but it still represented a lot of car for the money. The Town Landau was just under $8,000, but the cars made the right impact on the sales floor with over 318,000 being sold, a great success for Ford.

Essentially, the Thunderbird simply ran on for 1978 as no one wanted to mess with such sales success. There were trim changes as expected, and an extra model, the Diamond Jubilee Edition, that commemorated the 75th anniversary of the Ford company. It was expensive, at over $10,000, but for all that

19,000 were sold. For buyers seeking a reminder of the origins of the Thunderbird, there was a sports decor package option that was mainly composed of special trim items to enhance that aspect.

During the year a further model was, in effect, added to the range with the T-Roof Convertible Option. This was in the Targa form that offered some aspects of open-air motoring while retaining the comfort of the hardtop. To this end the roof panel between the windshield and the front of the Targa roof band was replaced by a narrow fixed member and a pair of removable glass panels that went into a storage bag when not fitted.

Sales went up further so the whole range ran on for 1979 with a revised front grille and twin taillights in place of the single assembly. Behind the scenes there was some drama with Lee Iacocca fired late in 1978 to go to Chrysler, as Henry Ford II thought that he had gathered too much power, much as Knudsen before him. For 1979 the special edition model was renamed the Heritage but with no real change, and some 284,000 cars were sold to bring the late-1970 period to a fine close. However, despite this three-year success, the times, legislation, and another oil embargo added up to recession and a time for the models for the next decade to make their debut.

Above: A single, full-width taillight assembly returned for the 1970 models, this the two-door Landau that was built along with the hardtop and the four-door Landau.

Overleaf: Little money was available for changes for 1971, but the grille, front bumper, and wheel covers were revised along with minor trim alterations, while the same three-model range was offered.

Small and Aero — 1980 to 1988

The new decade demanded that cars were more fuel efficient and the government drove that theme forward with a Corporate Average Fuel Economy program that was mandatory from 1980 onward. It simply meant that each US manufacturer had to achieve 20 mpg. or better from its complete line — and this figure was set to rise as the years went by. The legislation did not prohibit thirsty cars, it just meant that these had to be balanced out by really frugal ones.

The 1977 Thunderbird had looked down that road by losing some weight and size — but not enough. Another stringent diet was needed, and a good deal of attention paid to achieving greater efficiency from all areas. So the model went to a compact car platform and the wheelbase dropped to 108.4 inches, just six inches more than the first two-seater and less than the four-seater first seen in 1958.

Body construction changed back to unitary, with front and rear subframes, and the whole body shell was shorter but still with the bold, square front end of the past. The overall length went down by over two feet from the 1976 figure to just over 200 inches. The width reduced by

Right: A new body style was introduced for 1987 and saw the end of the front grille in most cases. Its form was sleeker and smoother than ever to cut down air drag and wind noise.

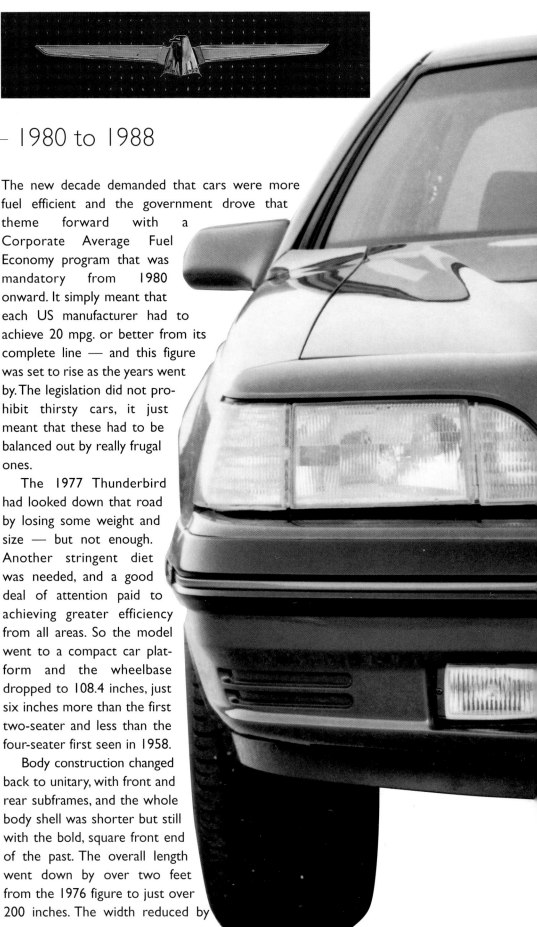

5.6 inches but this was not done by sacrificing interior space; in fact, this was increased as was the trunk capacity and rear seat legroom.

Wind resistance was another way to improve fuel consumption as well as the reduction in frontal area. Wind tunnel tests played their part, and a significant reduction in drag was made compared to the 1979 car. The final result had a rectangular grille flanked by similarly shaped panels that concealed the headlights and continued round and into the sides for the turn signals. The two-door body continued with something of the Targa style still there, although the rear quarter windows went while the side opera ones remained.

With less weight to haul and lower wind resistance to overcome, a smaller engine became the stock fitment and was the 255 cu. in. V-8 which produced 115 bhp. The 302 cu. in. engine continued as the option fit and was standard for a Silver Anniversary Edition built to celebrate 25 years of Thunderbird production. The other models were the Two-Door and Town Landau, and all had the option of a new transmission when fitted with the 302 cu. in. engine. Known as Automatic OverDrive, or AOD, this had four speeds with top an overdrive which boosted fuel economy and helped meet the government target figure.

Fixtures, fittings, and options were in the Thunderbird tradition, so all the models were well equipped, the Landau more so and the Anniversary with a special finish. Among the features to attract buyers was a keyless lock system with a keypad in the door, a digital dashboard for a high-tech look to the instruments, and better wheels and tires that improved handling already sharpened by the use of rack-and-pinion steering.

During the year a further engine option was added, an in-line six, a first of that type for the Thunderbird. Of 200 cu. in. and producing 88 bhp, it confirmed the determination to win the battle to save fuel. However, the box front style was perhaps too reminiscent of the heavy and thirsty cars of the 1970s and failed to catch on as another energy crisis hit the U.S. Sales went down with a thud to 156,000.

There were still three models for 1981, with the top one renamed the Heritage. For the first time in the history of the Thunderbird, a V-8 engine was not the standard fit, this job going to the 200 cu. in. in-line six for the Two-Door and Town Landau models. The 255 cu. in. V-8 became the stock unit for the Heritage and an option for the other two while the 302 cu. in. remained an option for all.

The AOD transmission was available with the V-8 engines but the base six only came with the usual three-speed automatic. To enhance the fuel economy aspect, a viscous clutch was added in the cooling fan drive so that it could idle at speed and not add under-hood drag. Later, the industry would adopt the thermostatic control of an electric motor for its cooling fans so that they only ran when needed and then at an optimum speed for their blade design.

On the outside, the front end for the 1981 model was amended in the area under the grille, while night driving was made easier by the adoption of halogen headlights. A fresh option for buyers who liked the style of a convertible but not the potential for drafts, leaks, or vandalism, was a simulated top that looked the part without the problems. The changes failed to have the desired effect and sales went down further to 86,000 — good by the standards of some years but poor by others.

It got worse before it got better, with the figure down to 45,000 in 1982 when another new engine type made its appearance, a 232 cu. in. V-6. The same range of models was offered with the 200 cu. in. in-line six the stock engine for the Two-Door and Town Landau and the V-6 optional, while the 255 cu. in. V-8 was stock for the Heritage and an option for the others. Both the V-6 and V-8 engines could be matched to the four-speed AOD transmission, while the three-speed automatic was improved and standard with both sizes.

There was little real change on the outside of the 1982 cars other than to the finish and trim. On the inside there were minor changes and a computer an option that gave a readout of fuel consumption and other data. A larger fuel tank increased the driving range between stops, with this aided by the improved economy, especially that of the V-6 engine.

The massive drop in sales called for some drastic thinking, and the results appeared in 1983 sitting on a 104-inch wheelbase. This made it just two inches up on the 1955 figure, just under 100 lb. heavier and less than an inch wider. It was a radical redesign in which wind tunnel hours played a key part in reducing the drag of the car by a substantial margin.

To this end the new body shell had a very different outline with the nose lower and running back to a well-raked windshield. The bumper line was taken round to the side to run all the way along the car to the rear, while the grille was smaller, laid back, and slightly rounded, although still of egg-crate form. It was flanked by a deep-set pair of headlights on each side, with the outer one set back more than the inner and the turn signals at the outer corner of each light housing. It was still a two-door body, but the opera windows had become full depth and their line a continuation of the main door windows.

Two models were listed at first, the basic Thunderbird and the deluxe Heritage, both powered by the 232 cu. in. V-6 engine and

Above: The Aero look brought no loss of performance although this 1986 picture shows a much modified car with the massive rear tires typical of drag racing.

fitted with the three-speed automatic transmission. As usual, the base model was well equipped, while the Heritage added further creature comforts and some electronic instruments in place of the usual dials.

It was a change of direction for the Thunderbird, away from the deep-pile carpet luxury of its recent years and more towards its earlier, more sporting days. This showed up in the response it met in the showroom, where its modern design, use of new technology, and trend-setting theme appealed more to the younger and technically sophisticated sections of the market. Those who preferred the square style of the past tended to be older but the real Thunderbird market had always been more sporting.

Early in the year a third model was added to the line as the Turbo Coupe. It was squarely aimed at the sporting end of the Thunderbird market. With it came several firsts for the series, beginning with the engine. This had four cylinders, an overhead camshaft, and a Garrett turbocharger, all new features to the Thunderbird and which helped it to generate 142 bhp. It was coupled to a five-speed manual gearbox driving a limited-slip differential in the rear axle, another first, with fifth gear being an overdrive. Other special features included modified suspension, better shock absorbers, different wheels and tires, front air dam with fog lights set in it and some changes to the trim.

At the same time the 302 cu. in. V-8 engine made a reappearance as an option for the cars normally fitted with the V-6, and

Ford was back in business with 122,000 sold that year. Around 12,000 were the Turbo Coupe, so that not only did it do well in its own right, it and its image also brought people into the showrooms and helped to sell both stock Thunderbirds and other Ford models.

It was minor changes for 1984, with the same three engines listed for four distinct models. Of these, the Thunderbird and Turbo Coupe ran on, while the Heritage was replaced by the Elan. The extra model was the Fila with a designer image and style that reflected the Italian sportswear firm. It was powered by the 232 cu. in. engine driving the AOD transmission, and was fitted with some items taken from the Turbo specification, others from the option list and had its own finish, paint lining, and badges. It was for a purchaser who wanted to make a statement and helped sales boom to 170,000.

The same four models continued for 1985, with the addition of a 30th Anniversary Edition. All had a new grille at the front and taillight for the rear, a counterbalance for the hood in place of the prop rod, and an improved finishing process to better combat corrosion. On the inside there were changes to the instrument panel, seats, and console, while the Turbo Coupe became available with automatic transmission. The 30th Anniversary Edition was offered from the start of the year and based on the Elan with a special color finish.

Sales had gone down to 152,000 in 1985 but were up again in 1986 to 164,000, when just three models were listed, the Fila

Above: The 1987 Turbo Coupe kept the 140 cu. in., overhead camshaft, four-cylinder engine but an added intercooler boosted power to 190 bhp. With this engine Ford insisted that purchasers had the five-speed manual gearbox.

being dropped. The engines continued as before, with fuel injection joining electronic ignition as the standard wear to improve efficiency and keep up with legislation requirements. The high-mounted brake stop light came on the scene, fine for warning the driver three cars back that traffic was halting, less so in traffic when it shone directly into following eyes.

While Ford itself had produced a number of special editions of the Thunderbird, there were other firms that built models based on the T'Bird and with approval from Ford. One such was Harry Shaw, who had begun to build replicas of the original 1955 Thunderbird in 1979, using a fiberglass body, a reproduction of the original frame, and a choice of the modern Ford engines. The replicas were built to a high standard and not offered as a kit, to ensure that this standard was kept to maintain the Ford blessing. They sold to buyers who wanted the style without the problems of finding and running an old car, and cost around the same as a well-restored original.

Another avenue was for the performance market, built by Roush Racing as the Mexican Grand Prix Thunderbird for the market in that country. The cars were powered by a turbocharged V-6 engine, had special wheels and tires, and aerodynamic aids to help keep these firmly in contact with the ground.

The Thunderbird line had the body further improved for 1987 with a number of drag reduction measures. At the front there was a much smaller grille, with the headlights and turn signals flush mounted to each side, and the whole blended in for better air penetration. This was continued by the use of flush-mounted glass to smooth the air flow along the body and over a redesigned roof that led to a new rear window and raised rear deck over the trunk. There were also changes to the taillight area, new side moldings, and new wheels, and the result did cut through the air more easily. Underneath, the handling was improved by refinements to the front suspension, while the interior had some trim changes.

Four models were listed for 1987, with the Elan replaced by the LX and joined by the Sport to run with the base model and Turbo Coupe. The Thunderbird continued with the 232 cu. in. V-6 engine as standard and the 302 cu. in. V-8 as the option, while the LX luxury version had the same choices. The stock model was a well-equipped car for the price ticket, but the LX had many items from the option list fitted as standard so was a fine buy for the customer seeking luxury in a two-door, trendy package.

The Thunderbird Sport was aimed at the other end of the market and, to suit this, came with the 302 cu. in. V-8 engine as standard with the AOD four-speed transmission as part of the package. It had some of the suspension improvements of the Turbo Coupe plus the limited-slip differential, bucket seats, and sports fittings and trims. At a whole new level there remained the Turbo Coupe, always a good car in its class, but transformed for 1987 to class leader. Under the hood there was still the 140 cu. in., overhead camshaft, turbocharged four, but this now incorporated an intercooler in the intake system to boost the power to 190 bhp. The intercooler was only fitted where the manual five-speed gearbox was used, so buyers using the AOD transmission had to settle for the lower output of 150 bhp.

More power was just the start for the Turbo Coupe, as with it came better stopping thanks to disc brakes and anti-lock on all four wheels. The handling was improved by an automatic ride control system that monitored various sensors for speed, steering, and suspension movements to adjust the shock absorber damping to suit. This also incorporated a manual switch to change from town to firm or sports mode as the driver required.

On the outside the Turbo Coupe differed from the other models as there was no front grille, so the space between the headlights was a plain panel. Twin air vents went into the hood to feed cold air to the intercooler, and under the bumper line went a deep air dam with twin night driving lights set in it. In addition to these features there was a special finish to many external details, a color band around the car, special badges, and alloy wheels with performance tires. It added up to a very impressive car out on the road and one available at a highly competitive price for what it offered and came with.

The long option list ran on and was joined by a line of Preferred Package Options. These comprised a list of the options for each model that could be ordered for a new car at a discount compared with the option price list. This gave the customer more car for the money, while it was easier for Ford to fit the items on the assembly line and ring up a few more dollars at the till. All of these things enabled Ford to build 128,000 that year.

All four models ran on for 1988, when production rose to 147,000, and apparently were little altered. However, the V-6 engine was revised and its power raised to 140 bhp thanks to its fuel injection. It was fitted with a balancer shaft that went in the vee between the cylinders and the purpose of this was to reduce the effect of vibrations felt by the occupants of the car.

Final decade, End, Restart — 1989 to 2000

For 1989 the Thunderbird was so altered and improved that it was more a new car than the tenth generation of the series. It made more efficient use of the space it occupied, and while the overall length went down, the wheelbase increased by nine inches. In addition, both front and rear tracks were enlarged, the front by over three inches, with little change in width. The net result was to move the wheels out towards the corners of the car, always a good way of improving road holding and handling. To further improve these attributes, the independent front suspension was revised and joined by independent rear suspension, a first for the Thunderbird.

On the outside more hours in the wind tunnel lessened the drag further and resulted in new lines and body panels from front to rear. Just about all items changed, and the outcome was a very sleek car that looked quite different from the previous version, although it still retained the lines and style of a Ford. There were three models and all used the 232 cu. in. V-6 engine so space under the hood was saved and the hood line lowered as the need to accommodate the V-8 was gone, the type being retired after many years of faithful service.

The 232 cu. in. engine was fine for the base Thunderbird and more luxurious LX models but not the third one, the Super Coupe, that replaced the Turbo. For that the engine remained the 232 cu. in. V-6 but with the addition of an engine-driven supercharger that boosted the power to 210 bhp. The Super took over many of the features of the Turbo, including the five-speed gearbox, all-round disc brakes with anti-lock, limited-slip differential, special suspension parts, aluminum wheels, performance tires and its own style of front air dam, plus side skirts between the wheels.

Right: The hood of the Super Coupe carried this marking so that cars ahead would know who wanted to get by them in a hurry, using one of the five manual gears.

Above: A 1990 Super Coupe against an interesting background, the car changing little from its introduction the previous year. The 210 bhp. was balanced by disc brakes all round.

These were all fine cars for the last decade of the century with the base model continuing to be well equipped by any standard, the LX with its many extras and the Super Coupe with its more than adequate performance. Little was altered for 1990 when a 35th Anniversary Edition celebrated another milestone for the series. It was based on the Super Coupe and had its own black and silver finish for both the outside and the interior.

It was back to three models for 1991 with minimal alterations, but popular demand brought the 302 cu. in. V-8 engine back from retirement as an option for the base and LX models. It proved a tight fit under the lower hood line, and getting it in meant changes which resulted in the loss of some of its power which came down to 200 bhp. Otherwise, there were few changes and these mainly to the interior trim.

Special Thunderbirds continued to be built by other firms with the Bill Elliott Ford Signature Edition Thunderbird being based on the LX with the 302 cu. in. V-8 engine and AOD transmission. Special wheels, front air dam, rear spoiler, and ground effect aids gave it a stylish line assisted by a bright red on white finish with gold stripes.

An alternative was a shortened, two-seat car that was tried by Ford in 1991 but found to be too expensive. However, two

private firms took this concept forward and the results were short-wheelbase, or SWB, Thunderbirds that retained the right looks. It meant cutting some eight inches out of the body but time and skill plus money brought this about in a highly professional manner.

For 1992 there was an extra model as the Sport returned to the range, and the Super Coupe front end style was used for all of them. There were minor differences but it became much harder to tell the models apart at a distance. The Sport was essentially the base Thunderbird fitted with the 302 cu. in. V-8, 200 bhp. engine under the hood and badged to suit. The LX and Super Coupe completed the line and were the only models to go forward for 1993.

The two models had little real change and continued to sell well so ran on for 1994, with the front end again revised to an even smoother form that was both simple and elegant. The interior was all new, with the areas in front of driver and passenger curled round each to separate them but without putting distance between them. This placed the instruments and controls, including those in the center console, nearer the driver and worked well. The stock engine continued to be the 232 cu. in. V-6 for the LX and the supercharged version for the Super Coupe with its

Above: Rear view of the Super Coupe with "Thunderbird SC" molded into the rear bumper to ensure you know what has just blasted past. Twin T'Bird badges on the rear lights to make sure of the message.

Above: Forty years apart, the first hard-top from 1955 (at top of photograph) and the svelte offering for 1995. Both were special cars in their way, standing some way apart from the usual run of sedans and showing some of the advances made in four decades.

power up to 230 bhp. An option for the LX was a new 280 cu. in. V-8 developing 205 bhp.

As the 1990s progressed, it seemed that the Thunderbird series had begun to run out of steam and that there was little more that could be done in the way of developing its personal luxury and performance image. After 1994 sales declined as there were few real changes to the cars and public taste took buyers elsewhere. Finally, at the end of 1997, the Thunderbird left the lists. It had flown its last, or so it seemed.

However, such a classic icon could not be allowed to fade away, and at the start of 1999 a new Ford Thunderbird concept car went on show in the U.S. In March it made its debut in Europe. It was back to the future with a vengeance, for it had an open, two-seater body, detachable hardtop with portholes, oval egg-crate mesh grille, air scoop on the hood, and circular taillights.

It was essentially a simple shape, but it managed to combine much of the essence of what the original Thunderbird had been about with modern ideas. Just one of the many details was the line from the top of each headlight that ran cleanly to the tail to suggest the fins of the past. Inside the cockpit were two bucket seats in black to go with the sunmist yellow of the body seen in the U.S. or the starlet red shown in Europe. The Thunderbird

badge was carried with pride for the concept was that of the simpler times when it had first been seen.

For all that, the new Thunderbird was to be totally modern in its design, technology, and equipment. It was to revive the ideas of a personal car, a sporting car, individual and one that set trends. A legend in it own lifetime, it was to return and fire the imagination of another generation of Americans.

Once more, Thunderbirds were go, ready for the new millennium.

Above: Ford went motor racing down the years in many ways, both in Europe and the U.S. By the late-1990s the company was heavily involved with **NASCAR** racing, as seen here in 1997.

Left: Two Thunderbirds at Indianapolis in 1997. Speeds at the Brickyard, as it was known, are always high at well over 200 mph. or 300 km/h.

Overleaf: The base and **LX** models had a different front end style to the Super Coupe, with fewer air ducts and simpler intakes to feed and cool the engine.

Restoration

The photographs on this and the next spread show restored vehicles in the Sarasota Classic Car, Florida Museum, where some 120 cars are joined by around 2,000 musical items ranging from hurdy gurdies to arcade machines. It is one of the oldest motor museums in the United States and part of the Bellm Cars & Music of Yesterday display. Note the simulated vent trim (Below Right); this was a feature from the start, but it was not joined by the name script until 1957, located on the tail fender for earlier cars.

Concours or clean runner, the beauty of the restoration market is that the choice is completely yours: but make the choice carefully. Rule one is not to attempt more than you will enjoy, or the pleasure will become a chore. A ground-up restoration job is not everyone's choice; many less-accomplished restorers will get just as much fun from readying a clean runner, or simply adding a few modern improvements to old suspension or electric systems to better cope with modern traffic.

You will need time, money, and equipment in varying degrees for any restoration. Rule two is to ensure that you don't take on a job that requires equipment you don't have or can't use. An honest assessment of your own capabilities is best made before you start. Few of us are experts at everything, so be selective: enjoy the electrics if that is your area, farm out the sheet metal if that is not.

Before you do anything else, learn your subject. Find out more about the Thunderbird and the different models, years, and options. Research sources of data, technical information, buyers guides, and road tests. Search out the clubs and the sources of parts. There are plenty available to cover most or all of your needs.

Remember that "complete, correct, and condition" applies to parts as well as cars and that it is often the smallest detail fittings that are the hardest to get right.

Most of all, make sure it stays fun.

Above: The Convertible Sports Roadster model was added to the Thunderbird line for 1962 by fixing a glass-fiber tonneau cover over the rear seats to take the car back to its two-seat origins.

Left: Rear quarter of the 1962 Convertible Sports Roadster on show in the museum. It retained the round style of the taillight from the original but this would change for 1964.

Opposite Page, Above: The space-age style of the 1962 Thunderbird was only seen for three years and in sharp contrast to the Squarebird one that preceeded it.

Opposite Page, Below: The bullet nose used for the cars from 1961 to 1963 retained the quad headlights first used in 1958 but in a fully revised style.

Above: Once you have restored
your T'bird you'll want to show it
off—and what better way to do so
than at a weekend show or cruise.
Most weekends in Old Town,
Orlando, Florida, see a Friday Nite
Cruise and Display for 1973 to 1987
cars and trucks, while the Saturday
Nite Cruise is devoted to older
vehicles for which this 1956
Thunderbird qualifies.

Right: Under the trunk lid much of
the space could be occupied by the
top when folded. A power top
means contacts, motors, limit
switches, and other details, all of
which have to work correctly and in
the right sequence. This is not a
straightforward job if you're poor
with electrics.

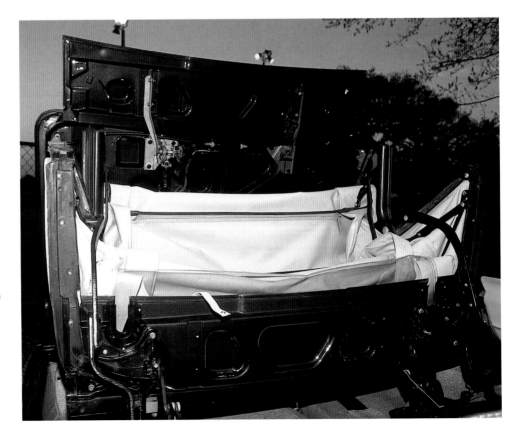

Above: Front end of the 1956 Thunderbird that had the air vents added in front of each door to help cool the passenger compartment. This one is out in Old Town, Orlando.

Left: The external continental carrier for the spare wheel was on option for 1955 but standard for 1956 to give more luggage space in the trunk. This was enlarged for 1957 to relieve the problem but the kit remained available.

A NEW BEGINNING?

Above: The Thunderbird was dropped from the lists at the end of 1997 but the firm had no intention of allowing such a classic icon to fade away. Early in 1999 a new concept car made its debut to pick up the old theme again.

Right: The rear of the concept car matched the front in looking to the past when twin round taillights were all the rage. Here, they complement the simple lines of the new Thunderbird to continue the original concept.